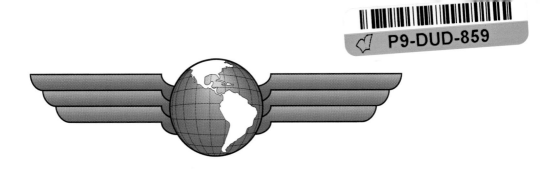

The First Flight Across the United States

The Story of Calbraith Perry Rodgers and His Airplane, the Vin Fiz

The First Flight Across the United States

**The Story of Calbraith Perry Rodgers and
His Airplane, the Vin Fiz**

by Richard L. Taylor

Franklin Watts
New York / London / Toronto / Sydney
A First Book

Photographs copyright ©: Cover (clouds): John Chard/Tony Stone Images; Cover (Vin Fiz): 6, 29 (bottom), 33, 36, 36–37, 41 (bottom), 57, 61: UPI/Bettmann; 8–9, 9 (bottom), 10 (top), 10–11, 12, 14–15, 15 (bottom), 25 (top), 26–27: Culver Pictures; 18: no credit; 21, 26, 56: The Bettmann Archives; 25 (bottom): Chicago Historical Society; 29 (top), 32, 34, 39 52–53, 59: National Air and Space Museum; 35: Courtesy Richard G. Loder; 40–41, 44–45: Courtesy of Betsy Mathis, Wooster, Ohio, photo by Harold Foelak; 48: National Air and Space Museum, photo by Harold Foelak; 49 (top and bottom): no credit; 53 (top): Tournament of Roses Association, Pasadena, CA

Library of Congress Cataloging-in-Publication Data
Taylor, Richard L.
The first flight across the United States : the story of Calbraith Perry Rodgers and his airplane, the Vin Fiz / by Richard L. Taylor.
p. cm. — (A First book)
Includes bibliographical references (p.) and index.
Summary: A biography of the pioneering aviator, trained by the Wright brothers, who completed the first flight across the United States in 1911.
ISBN 0-531-20159-7 (lib. bdg.)
1. Rodgers, Calbraith Perry—Juvenile literature. 2. Air pilots—United States—Biography—Juvenile literature. 3. Vin Fiz (Airplane)—Juvenile literature. 4. Aeronautics—United States—Flights—Juvenile literature. [1. Rodgers, Calbraith Perry. 2. Air pilots. 3. Vin Fiz (Airplane)] I. Title. II. Series.
TL540.R576T38 1993
629.13'092—dc20
[B]   93-6881
        CIP
        AC

Contents

The Prize and the Problems

"Welcome aboard Flight 703, ladies and gentlemen. Our flight time to Los Angeles will be six hours and fifteen minutes, at a cruising altitude of thirty-nine thousand feet. Please sit back, relax, and enjoy the flight." That's a typical announcement heard by the passengers on a jet airliner departing New York City on its way to the west coast.

Transcontinental flights have become routine. Many times each day, airliners leave major cities on the east and west coasts, carrying thousands of passengers nonstop to the other side of the country. These flights are not only fast, but they are comfortable, safe, and almost always depart and arrive on time. Many of us take for granted the reliability of today's air transportation. It hasn't always been like that. In 1804, President Thomas Jefferson sent two explorers, Meriwether Lewis and William Clark, to find out what lay beyond the Rocky Mountains. They traveled by boat, on horseback,

7

on foot, and finally reached the Pacific Ocean two years later. Settlers who went west in wagon trains were able to make the trip in a matter of months, and as railroads spread out across the land, transcontinental travel time was reduced even more. The first coast-to-coast crossing by automobile took place in 1903. That trip required sixty-five days.

An exciting new mode of transportation appeared in 1903, when the Wright brothers made the first successful airplane flight. It would be many years, however,

(top left) **Aviation in the United States began at Kitty Hawk, North Carolina, with the Wright Brothers first flight in 1903.**
(lower right) **In the beginning, preparation for flight often took longer than the actual flying time.**

TAKING THE WRIGHT AEROPLANE FROM ITS SHED.

before air transportation would become practical. Even five years later, the Wrights were pleased when they could stay aloft for an hour and fly at the astounding (for 1908) speed of 40 miles (64 km) per hour.

But fly all the way across the country? Most people considered it a success if an airplane could fly all the way across town. Traveling from one coast to the other by air was unheard of in 1908.

Aviation technology had not made great leaps between 1903 and the beginning of World War I in 1914. The Wright brothers were the ones who best knew how to build and fly an airplane, and they kept their secrets to themselves. The airplanes that others built were not much better than the original Wright Flyer, an airplane that was incapable of long trips.

The struggle to improve airplanes and flight moved slowly between 1908 and 1914. These photos of pre-World War I planes show two attempts at improvement.

Although airplanes were rickety, slow, and undependable, they were the most spectacular thing people had seen in those years before World War I. A good horse could run 20 miles (32 km) per hour, and some cars could do 30 to 40 miles (48 to 64 km) per hour, but an airplane could beat both of them — and frequently did, as part of the "aerial circuses" that toured the country.

William Randolph Hearst was a wealthy California newspaper publisher who believed in aviation and wanted to show that airplanes could be useful instead of merely serving as sensational attractions in air circuses. He offered a $50,000 prize to the first aviator who could fly from one coast to the other in thirty days or less. The flight could be made in either direction along a route of the pilot's choice, as long as he made a stop in Chicago.

William Randolph Hearst

Sixty days would have been a more reasonable time limit. It appeared that flying from one side of the United States to the other was simply a matter of putting together enough short flights to equal the total distance. But to do it in thirty days would require at least ten or twelve hours of flying every day for a month, and there were neither pilots nor airplanes able to do that. In 1911, flights of more than one hour without mechanical problems were rare.

Those early airplanes were frail machines. They were built entirely of wood, with cloth-covered wings. The engines overheated and broke down frequently. Even when the engines ran their smoothest, they shook the entire airplane so much that the mechanics frequently had to tighten and adjust the wires that held the whole structure together. And when an airplane crashed (as most of them did, sooner or later), it usually wound up as a pile of broken sticks, crumpled fabric, and twisted wires.

A pilot entering the Hearst race would need a ground crew to provide supplies and repair damage to his airplane. The only way to do this was by rail, and so the contestants arranged for special trains to follow them across the country.

The railroads also solved the problem of navigation—knowing where to go. Thousands of miles of railroads crisscrossed the country, and a pilot who followed the right set of tracks could find his way from New York

(top) **Early air expositions often ended in crashes, reflecting the imperfection of early aviation technology.**
(left) **Despite the danger, early aviators persisted in thrilling the public with new and varied displays of daring.**

to California. This worked out especially well because the pilots would have to stay close to their supply trains.

Then there was the matter of human endurance. The airplanes available in 1911 were very unstable. They tended to move about in all directions, and the pilot found himself making continuous adjustments with the flight controls. With no time to relax, a pilot would tire very quickly — to say nothing of sitting on a very uncomfortable chair for several hours each day, fully exposed to wind, rain, and cold.

The first transcontinental flight was an enormous challenge to pilots and airplanes alike. Nevertheless, seven aviators indicated that they would try for the Hearst prize. Only three of them actually began the trip, and only one finished.

Cal Rodgers Learns to Fly

Galbraith Perry Rodgers was 6 feet 4 inches (1.9 m) tall, a good athlete, and very strong-willed. Once he decided to do something, nothing could keep him from finishing the job.

Cal Rodgers would most likely have entered the U.S. Naval Academy and followed a family tradition of military service. But he was stricken with scarlet fever at age six, and the disease damaged his hearing and his sense of balance. A naval career was out of the question.

After just one year at a prep school in Pennsylvania, Cal came to the conclusion that further studies were a waste of his time. He withdrew from the academy, moved to New York City, and turned his attention to motorcycles, boats, and automobiles. He enjoyed driving any kind of vehicle, and the faster it went, the better he liked it.

In 1911, Rodgers (now thirty-two years old) was invited to visit his cousin, John Rodgers, at the Wright

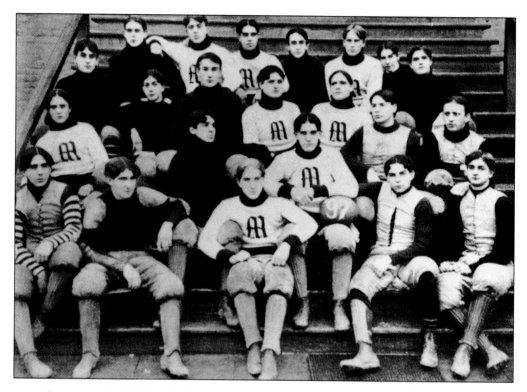

Strong and athletic, Cal Rodgers played on the 1894 Mercersburg football team. Cal is in the third row, second from the left.

brothers' flying school in Dayton, Ohio. John was one of the first naval aviators and was assigned to the Wright school for training.

Cal was thunderstruck by the flying machines he saw in Dayton. His wife, Mabel, said, "It was as if the last piece of a jigsaw puzzle had dropped into place in his mind."

Less than two months later, Cal was back in Dayton, ready to enroll as a student. Flying lessons cost sixty dollars per hour and were given in fifteen-minute units. A student's training program was considered complete when he could take off and land safely by himself.

Cal's first lessons were on the ground. The Wright brothers wanted to make sure their students understood how airplanes were built and maintained. Cal was also taught the principles of flight — how lift and thrust are created and managed, how to make turns in the air, how to take off and land an airplane.

Next was a session on the "kiwi," a training device named for a bird that cannot fly. The kiwi was an airplane without an engine, wings, or tail, mounted so that an electric motor tilted it from side to side. When the student operated the flight controls properly, the wings returned to level. The kiwi helped students to develop instinctive reactions with the controls before a student tried to fly a real airplane. Cal overcame his balance problem and quickly mastered the kiwi. He was ready for his first flight.

Wright Model B airplanes were used for training. They were bigger, more powerful, and easier to control than the Wrights' 1903 Flyer, the world's first true airplane. The Model B had a 35-horsepower engine, rear-

19

mounted elevators and rudder, and two seats. Instead of the skids and launching rail used to get the Flyer into the air, the Model B had wheels so that it could take off and land on grass fields.

A lever between the pilot seats operated the warping controls, which twisted the wings to bank and therefore turn the airplane. The pilot pushed forward on the lever to turn left, pulled back to turn right. The rudder was connected to the wing-warping lever and automatically assisted in turns.

On the outside of each pilot seat was a lever that controlled the elevators. Positioned at the rearmost part of the airplane, the elevators caused the nose to move up or down to change altitude.

This flight-control arrangement required the constant use of both hands, so a pedal between the seats was connected to the sparking system of the engine to provide control of engine speed.

Power from the four-cylinder engine was transmitted by bicycle chains to a pair of 8-foot (2.4-m) wooden propellers. One of the chains was crossed in a long figure eight so that the propellers turned in opposite directions and canceled each other's twisting force.

John Rodgers warned his cousin that there was nothing like flying, and Cal's first flight proved him right.

By 1910, flight schools, such as the Curtiss Flying School in Hammondsport, New York, sprouted up around the country.

His instructor demonstrated a takeoff and several turns around the converted cow pasture that served as a flying field. Some students were badly frightened and completely bewildered by their first experience in the air, but not Cal Rodgers. At the end of the flight he was ready to go again.

Six flights and ninety minutes of instruction later, Cal felt he was ready to fly solo. His instructor disagreed, not because Cal couldn't fly safely by himself, but because the Wrights didn't permit solo flights in company airplanes. So Cal bought the airplane. The Wright brothers had no rules that prevented a pilot from flying his own airplane by himself.

Rodgers' first solo flight lasted ten minutes, and when he landed, his heart was still in the sky. He later wrote to his wife, "Once you have left the ground to fly through the air, you never quite come down to earth again." Cal Rodgers would never again be satisfied with boats or automobiles — he was now an aviator.

Through the rest of June 1911, Cal practiced the maneuvers he'd been taught, then began an aerial exhibition tour with his cousin John. The two pilots put on flying shows throughout western Ohio, swooping low over the crowds, dipping and turning, dropping mock bombs, and racing against automobiles.

Having decided to earn a living with his airplane, Rodgers' next step was to obtain a license. He could continue flying without one, but a license would admit him to major air meets without paying an entrance fee. A license was also a mark of respect and prestige among fellow pilots.

On August 7, Cal passed the test and became the world's forty-ninth licensed pilot.

Preparing for the Race

The Chicago International Aviation Meet of 1911 was billed as the "Greatest Event in the History of Aeronautics." It attracted aviators from Europe and Great Britain as well as the United States.

The meet included contests for speed, distance, and duration, and a new record of some sort was established almost every time a pilot took to the air. Cal Rodgers set his sights on the duration prize, and when the nine-day meet closed, he had won it with a total flying time of twenty-seven hours and sixteen seconds.

Rodgers was now convinced he could fly across the country and win the Hearst prize. He put together a small organization to manage the details, then headed for Dayton to talk with the Wrights about building an airplane that could make the trip.

Orville Wright wasn't very enthusiastic. He told Cal, "There isn't a machine in existence that can be relied on for 1,000 miles, and here you want to go over 4,000.

It will vibrate itself to death before you get to Chicago."

Nevertheless, the Wrights came up with the "EX", a modified Model B biplane. It was slightly smaller, considerably lighter, and somewhat faster than the Model B. Its engine had only two speeds — wide open and off — but that didn't matter, because Rodgers intended to fly as fast as he could all the way across the country.

The Chicago International Aviation Meet in 1911, along the shores of Lake Michigan, drew visitors from across North America as well as Europe.

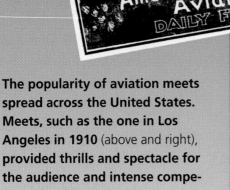

The popularity of aviation meets spread across the United States. Meets, such as the one in Los Angeles in 1910 (above and right), provided thrills and spectacle for the audience and intense competition for the aviators.

While Cal was arranging for the new airplane, his business manager was finalizing a contract with the Armour Company, a Chicago firm that had recently introduced a grape-flavored soft drink they called "Vin Fiz." They agreed to sponsor the trip in return for advertising their product.

The Wright EX was therefore named the *Vin Fiz,* and became a flying billboard. "Vin Fiz — The Ideal Grape Drink" was painted on the underside of the lower wing for all to see as the airplane flew overhead.

Armour agreed to provide the special railroad train, and pay Rodgers five dollars for every mile he flew east of the Mississippi River, but only four dollars a mile for the western part of the flight — there were fewer people out there to buy Vin Fiz.

The supply train, which came to be known as "The Vin Fiz Special," was one of a kind. It consisted of a steam locomotive and tender (a supply car carrying water for the engine), a private Pullman car for the Rodgers family (Cal's wife and mother went along), and a day coach for Armour personnel and the press.

The car coupled between the tender and the Pullman was the real attention-getter. It was, according to the lettering on its all-white sides, the "Aeroplane Car — Accompanying C.P. Rodgers — The Vin Fiz Flyer —

In return for sponsoring Rodgers on his journey, the Armour Company distributed thousands of broadsides (right) to audiences and followed the airplane across the United States with a brightly painted railroad car.

The Drink Above All

VIN FIZ, the new grape drink, is sweeping the country. Mr. Cal P. Rodgers is carrying its fame from coast to coast. It has won quick favor as the ONE BEST DRINK for all all-year 'round.
TRY ONE GLASS of the new sensation

VIN FIZ
REGISTERED TRADE MARK

Enjoy its delightful, delicious flavor; then you will understand its wonderful popularity.
At All Drinking Places
5c
Dispensers and Bottlers — Get full information

Made by
VIN-FIZ COMPANY
Lock Box 612
CHICAGO, ILL.

5¢   SOLD EVERYWHERE
VIN FIZ
REGISTERED TRADE MARK
THE IDEAL GRAPE DRINK

AEROPLANE CAR
ACCOMPANYING C. P. RODGERS IN T
VIN FIZ
FLYER
NEW YORK to CALIFORNIA

Competing for the Hearst $50,000 Prize — New York to California." This "hangar car" contained a machine shop, tools, spare parts, and living quarters for the mechanics. There was also room for Cal's own Model B airplane (disassembled, of course), and an automobile to shuttle people and parts when Cal couldn't land close to the train.

Late in the afternoon of Sunday, September 17, Rodgers arrived at the Sheepshead Bay race track on Long Island. The *Vin Fiz* had been thoroughly checked, the Vin Fiz Special was waiting in the railroad yard at Jersey City, just across the river from New York, and everything appeared ready. The first coast-to-coast flight was about to begin.

The Race Is On

When Cal Rodgers left the ground at Sheepshead Bay, he joined two other contestants for the Hearst prize.

Robert Fowler departed from San Francisco in a Wright biplane on September 11, and crashed while trying to cross the Sierra Nevada Mountains. He eventually made it to Jacksonville, Florida, but it took him 149 days to get there.

The other competitor was Jimmy Ward, who had taken off from New York on September 13 in a Curtiss airplane. A series of crashes caused him to withdraw from the race before he got out of New York state.

Rodgers climbed into the pilot's seat at 4:25 that Sunday afternoon, turned his cap around backwards, and adjusted his goggles. When he was certain the engine was running properly, he signaled the ground crew, "Let 'er go!" and guided the *Vin Fiz* into the air. Cal turned west, threw out a handful of Vin Fiz leaflets, and headed for Jersey City.

(top) **Rodgers took off on his trip west from Sheepshead Bay, New York, at 4:25 p.m., Sunday, September 17, 1911.** (right) **Cal Rodgers posed for cameras before beginning his historic trip from Brooklyn, New York, to California.**

Long strips of white cloth were fastened between the rails of the main line to help Rodgers identify the tracks he should follow. Cal spotted the markers and the special train and headed northwest for Middletown, New York, where he landed one hour and forty-five minutes later. The first lap of the cross-country flight was safely completed.

Rodgers was ready to go early the next morning, prepared to fly all day if necessary to make up for Sunday's late start. During the takeoff, the tail of the *Vin Fiz* tangled with the upper branches of a willow tree, and the airplane slammed to the ground. The only damage to the pilot was a sprained ankle and a cut forehead, but the airplane was nearly destroyed.

Rodgers' crew worked around the clock to get the airplane ready to fly. Three days later, with much of its structure repaired or replaced, the *Vin Fiz* was in the air again.

Rodgers first takeoff from Middletown, New York, ended in a crash as the *Vin Fiz*'s tail became tangled in tree branches (above). At left, a young local gives Rodgers a hand hauling the plane into a hangar for repairs.

Cal constantly checked the *Vin Fiz*'s engine to be sure that all was in order (above).
(right) The *Vin Fiz* slowly climbs during one of the many takeoffs on its slow advance west to California.

On the way to Hancock, New York, a spark plug failed, and Cal was forced to land. The right skid hit a soft spot in the field and snapped off, once again grounding the airplane until the train could catch up.

Foggy weather delayed the next day's takeoff until almost noon. Then Cal got lost. He landed in the first smooth field he saw and found out that he was near Scranton, Pennsylvania. Two stops later, Rodgers landed at Elmira, New York, and called it a day.

The takeoff next morning was a near-disaster. The ground was soft, the wind was light, and the *Vin Fiz* used three times the normal distance to get into the air. Rodgers climbed steeply to clear a tree, then saw telegraph wires directly ahead. The only choice was to land, and the impact pulled out some of the brace wires under the left wing.

A group of Elmira citizens carried the airplane to a better field, the wires were adjusted, and Cal was airborne shortly after 2 P.M. But then the engine began misfiring, and the *Vin Fiz* came to earth again. This time it was more of a controlled crash than a landing, and the lower left wing was completely crumpled. The mechanics worked all night to repair the damage.

Rodgers was underway at 10:13 A.M. the next day, and encountered a strong headwind. The *Vin Fiz* took

All along the route, local citizens enthusiastically helped Rodgers and the *Vin Fiz.* Here, citizens in Elmira, New York, move the plane to a better takeoff site. The tree in the background was nearly disastrous.

Cal Rodgers stopped in Marion, Ohio, to accept gratefully a cash prize from the town. Cal took off from Marion in slow, wide circles, waving to the townspeople below. (right) Rodgers buttons his jacket in preparation for yet another takeoff.

two hours and thirteen minutes to get to Olean, New York — a speed of only 29 miles (46 km) per hour across the ground.

After a quick lunch, Rodgers took off and headed for Jamestown, New York. The engine's electrical system began acting up again, and Cal landed in a meadow near the town of Salamanca. The problem was soon fixed, but when Rodgers tried to take off, the long grass kept the airplane from rolling fast enough to get into the air. A second attempt was also unsuccessful.

On the third try, Cal tried to make the *Vin Fiz* jump away from the grass and into the air, but there simply wasn't enough speed. The airplane crashed through two barbed-wire fences and came to a stop. The propellers were shattered, the wings, struts, skids, and control wires were demolished. There was nothing to do but load the wreckage on a flatcar and haul it back to town for repairs. It would be four more days before the *Vin Fiz* would fly again.

Rodgers finally resumed his flight on Thursday morning. A tailwind increased his groundspeed to a mile a minute, and Cal was able to fly all the way to Kent, Ohio, with only two stops for oil and fuel. It was his best day so far — 203 miles in 210 minutes, and most important, there was no damage to the *Vin Fiz*.

A day of bad weather and another crash on takeoff from Huntington, Indiana, kept Rodgers from reaching Chicago until October 8. It was now three weeks since leaving New York — three times as long as Rodgers had planned for that part of the trip. Worse, the $50,000 prize offer would expire in two days. There was no way the *Vin Fiz* could reach California in time to win.

A reporter asked Cal if he were going to quit the race, and he replied, "I'm going to do this whether I get $50,000 or fifty cents or nothing. I am going to cross this continent simply to be the first to cross in an aeroplane." And that was that. Cal Rodgers was not one to give up.

Another crash, this one in Huntington, Indiana, meant long hours of repair and reconstruction to get the *Vin Fiz* back in the air and on its journey.

On to California

Cal had made the required stop in Chicago a short one. Within a couple of hours, he was on his way to California.

Rodgers left Chicago on October 8, heading south, then west for Kansas City, Missouri, as the time limit for the Hearst prize ran out. He wasn't going to win $50,000, but he had flown farther than anyone else in the world — 1,398 miles (2,237 km) — and he was determined to go the rest of the way.

The *Vin Fiz* continued on its way south through Missouri, Oklahoma, and Texas, stopping to put on exhibitions in many of the small towns along the way.

There had been no serious accidents since the wreck in Huntington, Indiana, but the airplane was beginning to show the strain of a flight for which it was never intended. The chief mechanic said that things "were going from bad to worse after leaving Kansas City, and we were constantly repairing something about the ship."

On the afternoon of October 29, Cal stopped in Austin, the capital of Texas, where thousands of people had their first look at an airplane. He had taken off and was on his way to San Antonio when he heard a snap and felt a strong jolt. The engine was jumping up and down in its mounts, and Rodgers landed immediately in a cotton field.

The special train was close by, and the mechanics were soon looking for the problem. They discovered that one of the engine's valves had crystallized, a sure sign of a machine being pushed beyond its limits. The spare engine was installed, and the *Vin Fiz* was ready to go again the next morning.

Rodgers landed at San Antonio, Texas, on Sunday, October 22. From here, he would head west for the Pacific. Although the southern route across New Mexico and Arizona avoided the highest mountains, there was plenty of rough, desert country ahead. The scheduled departure was moved back one full day to give the mechanics time for a complete inspection of the *Vin Fiz*. They overhauled the engine and replaced a number of badly worn wires.

A few miles west of San Antonio, the electrical system failed. Rodgers landed, the mechanics made adjustments, and the *Vin Fiz* continued westward. Cal gave

Rodgers "buzzed" the Amicable Building in Waco on his trek across Texas.

exhibitions in Sabinal and Uvalde, and landed near Spofford, Texas, late in the afternoon.

The mechanics cleared a takeoff path alongside the railroad track for the next morning's takeoff. Just before the *Vin Fiz* left the ground, the right propeller hit a small mound of earth. The airplane swerved violently and crashed back to the ground. Rodgers wasn't hurt, but both propellers were splintered, the left wing was crumpled, and the skids were demolished. The *Vin Fiz* would have to be rebuilt one more time.

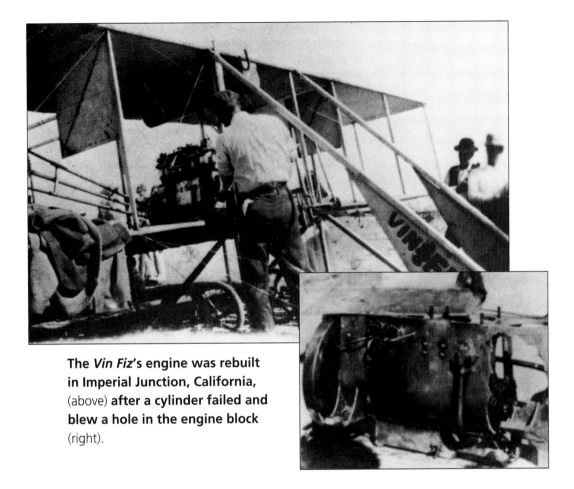

The *Vin Fiz*'s engine was rebuilt in Imperial Junction, California, (above) **after a cylinder failed and blew a hole in the engine block** (right).

During the second takeoff from Spofford, a gust of wind struck the *Vin Fiz* and Cal couldn't keep from crashing into a fence that bordered the field. The damaged left wing was repaired before the day was over, and Rodgers flew to El Paso, the last overnight stop in Texas.

Continuing his battle with the weather, a worn-out engine, and a weary airplane, Rodgers crossed New

Mexico and Arizona and flew into California on Friday, November 3. He was sailing along at 4,000 feet (1,219 m) near Imperial Junction when one of the cylinders failed and blew a hole in the side of the engine. Steel splinters flew in all directions. Several hit Cal's right arm, but he managed to get the *Vin Fiz* safely on the ground.

The mechanics were able to patch up the engine, but the rest of the airplane was in need of serious repairs. Mabel Rodgers summed it up: "The engine was belching double the amount of oil it was supposed to. The cloth on the wings was soaking wet with dirty oil. The four longerons [frames] holding the tail surface together had been pieced with twine and glue. The wire, all corroded, had turned greenish, the chains had secondhand bearings. We prayed that both Cal and his tired machine would be able to hold out."

Next Stop, Pasadena

The airplane was ready to fly again two days later, although everyone knew it was barely safe to fly. Nevertheless, Pasadena was only a little more than 200 (322 km) miles away, and Rodgers was determined to get there as soon as he could.

Just as the *Vin Fiz* reached the summit of San Gorgonio Pass the engine began to misfire, then it quit altogether. Cal was able to land in a plowed field; he discovered major engine problems that required another day to repair.

Less than 5 miles (8 km) after the next takeoff, the *Vin Fiz* was on the ground again, this time because the line from the gasoline tank had come loose. Cal repaired the line himself and flew on to Pomona, where he refueled and prepared for the final leg of the trip. One of his mechanics warned Rodgers that the airplane was in such bad condition that he should not fly the machine any further. Rodgers replied, "This machine has carried

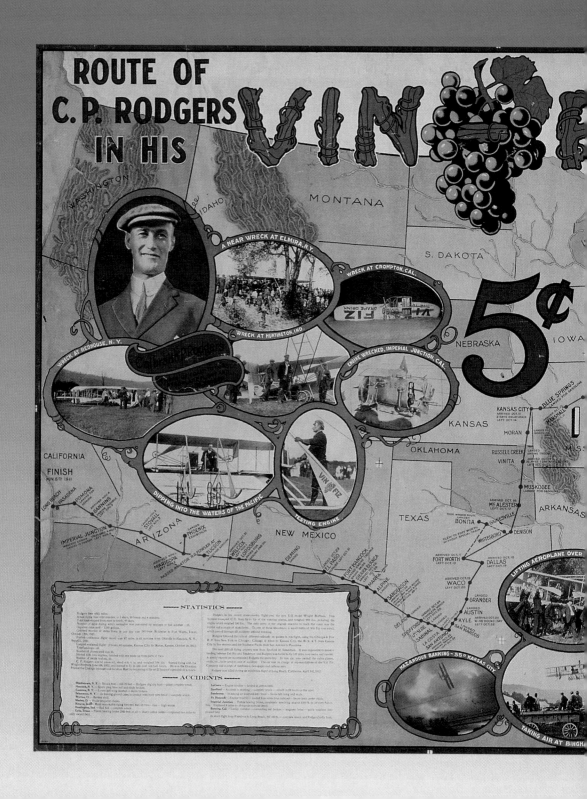

ROUTE OF
C. P. RODGERS
IN HIS VIN FIZ

5¢

A NEAR WRECK AT ELMIRA, N.Y.

WRECK AT CROMPTON, CAL.

WRECK AT HUNTINGTON, IND.

WRECK AT REDHOUSE, N.Y.

ENGINE WRECKED, IMPERIAL JUNCTION, CAL.

DIPPING INTO THE WATERS OF THE PACIFIC

TESTING ENGINE

LIFTING AEROPLANE OVER

HAZARDOUS BANKING - 55° KANSAS CITY

TAKING AIR AT BINGH...

━━ STATISTICS ━━

━ ACCIDENTS ━

WORLD'S RECORD FLIGHT FROM COAST to COAST

MICHIGAN

NEW YORK

MASSACHUSETTS

CONN

SALAMANCA

MEADVILLE

HANCOCK

MIDDLETOWN

SCRANTON

NEW JERSEY

CHICAGO

WARREN

KENT

HAMMOND

MARION

MANSFIELD

PENNSYLVANIA

HUNTINGTON

DRIVER

MARYLAND

GENEVA

OHIO

WEST VIRGINIA

VIRGINIA

THE

KENTUCKY

AL DRINK

(left) **The long, circuitous route of the *Vin Fiz* is traced in this promotional map distributed by the Armour Company.**
(above, right) **A triumphant Cal Rodgers is wrapped in an American flag and given a bouquet of flowers from Mrs. R.D. Davis, wife of the president of the Pasadena, California, Board of Trade.**

AUTO THRU STREETS OF HUNTINGTON

WRECK AT MIDDLETOWN, N.Y.

WRECK AT HUNTINGTON, IND.

THE AIR-START AT SHEEPSHEAD BAY

REPAIRING WRECK AT MIDDLETOWN, N.Y.

5¢

VIN FIZ

THE IDEAL GRAPE DRINK

VIN FIZ FLYER

NEW YORK to CALIFORNIA

me for more than four thousand miles. Now if I have to, I'll carry it." And off he went, bound for Pasadena.

Even though Pasadena is 20 miles (32 km) from the California coastline, it had been chosen as the official end of the first flight across the United States. A grand affair was planned for the thousands of people who wanted to see Cal Rodgers, the aviator who had flown all the way from New York. The newspaper suggested that citizens "throw business cares aside tomorrow afternoon and give the birdman a hearty welcome." Rodgers finally landed in Pasadena forty-nine days after he left New York.

One of the mechanics kept track of repairs throughout the trip. His records showed that the airplane that reached Pasadena was not the same airplane that had left New York. Eighty landings (many of them crashes) and eighty-two hours of flying had used up eight propellers, six sets of wings, two radiators, two complete engines, four propeller chains, and more struts and skids than anyone could count.

So many parts had been replaced and rebuilt that only the vertical rudder and the engine drip pan remained of the original *Vin Fiz*.

The following Sunday, November 12, Cal took off from Tournament Park and headed for Long Beach, 23 miles (37 km) away. He felt the trip wouldn't be complete until he actually reached the shore of the Pacific Ocean. No sooner was he headed west than the gasoline feed line broke again. Another forced landing, another quick repair.

The engine was hard to start, and Rodgers spent a long time on the ground trying to make it run properly. He knew it wasn't very dependable, but he took off anyway, not wanting to disappoint the large crowd gathered at Long Beach.

Fifteen minutes later the engine sputtered and quit, and this time Cal's luck ran out. He lost control and the *Vin Fiz* plummeted into a plowed field, throwing Rodgers headfirst into the mud. The gas tank broke loose and pinned him to the ground, the engine landed on his legs, and the rest of the airplane folded around him. Cal was alive, but he was seriously injured.

It was a full month before he was able to fly the remaining 12 miles (19 km) to complete the trip. He landed on the beach, shut down the engine and sat proudly in his pilot's seat as the *Vin Fiz* was pushed a few feet into the water. The first transcontinental flight was finished.

Rodgers intended to stay in California and eventually start his own airplane manufacturing business. In the

Cal Rodgers was killed in this crash at Long Beach, California, on April 13, 1912.

meantime, he used his original airplane (the Wright Model B in which he learned to fly) to give rides and exhibitions.

On April 3, Cal heard an unusual sound from the engine during a passenger flight at Long Beach. He landed, checked what he could, and decided to make a short test hop before flying with another customer.

He was flying along the beach just offshore when he spotted a flock of seagulls and dipped to avoid them. Then something went wrong, and the airplane plunged straight into the ocean. Some said that the engine quit, others claimed that a seagull had collided with the airplane and jammed the flight controls. Whatever the reason for the crash, Cal died instantly when the engine broke loose and shot forward, breaking his neck.

Two years later, Cal's mother wanted to have the *Vin Fiz* restored but she couldn't raise the money. The airplane was partially rebuilt for the 1933 Chicago International Exhibition, then was transferred to the Smithsonian Institution. The airplane now on display in the Smithsonian's National Air and Space Museum in Washington is a faithful recreation of the original.

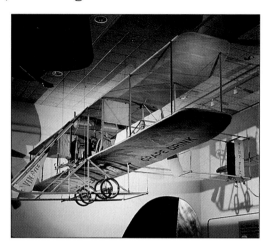

The restored *Vin Fiz* hangs today at the National Air and Space Museum in Washington, D.C.

Calbraith Perry Rodgers, pilot of the *Vin Fiz* and the first person to cross the United States in an airplane, is buried in Pittsburgh, Pennsylvania, under a 6-foot 4-inch (1.9 m) tombstone bearing the inscription "I conquer, I endure."

Facts, Figures, Important Dates

Calbraith Perry Rodgers

Born January 12, 1879 Pittsburgh, Pennsylvania

Died March 17, 1912 Long Beach, California

The Vin Fiz, a Wright Type EX biplane

Weight — 903 pounds (410 kg)

Wingspan — 31 feet 6 inches (9.6 m)

Length — 21 feet 5 inches (6.5 m)

Top speed — 55 miles per hour (88.5 km/h)

Engine — Four cylinder, four cycle, water cooled,
    35 horsepower at 1,325 rpm

Gasoline capacity — 15 gallons (3 $\frac{1}{2}$ hours flight time)

The First Flight Across the United States

Started — Sheepshead Bay, New York
    September 17, 1911

Ended — Long Beach, California, December 10, 1911

Statistics (best estimates; no accurate log was kept)

Total distance flown — 4,231 miles (6,809 km)

Actual flying time — 82 hours, 4 minutes

Average speed — 51.56 miles per hour (83 km/h)

Total time, New York to Long Beach — 84 days

Greatest distance flown in one day — 234 miles (377 km)

Longest single flight — 2 hours, 40 minutes

Longest single leg — 133 miles (214 km)

Gasoline used — 1,230 gallons (4,656 liters)

For Further Reading

Ault, Phil. *By the Seat of Their Pants: The Story of Early Aviation.* New York: Dodd, Mead, 1978.

Friedman, Russell. *The Wright Brothers: How They Invented the Airplane.* New York: Holiday House, 1991.

Hayman, LeRoy. *Aces, Heroes, and Daredevils of the Air.* New York: Julian Messner, 1981.

Jeffris, David. *The First Flyers: Pioneers of Aviation.* New York: Franklin Watts, 1988.

Jeffris, David. *Flight: Fliers and Flying Machines.* New York: Franklin Watts, 1991.

Prendergast, Curtis. *The First Aviators.* Alexandria, VA: Time-Life Books, 1980.

Taylor, Richard L. *The First Flight: The Story of the Wright Brothers.* New York: Franklin Watts, 1990.

Zisfein, Melvin B. *Flight: A Panorama of Aviation.* New York: Knopf, 1981.

Index

About the Author

Richard L. Taylor is an Associate Professor Emeritus in the Department of Aviation at the Ohio State University, having retired in 1988 after twenty-two years as an aviation educator. At retirement, he was the Director of Flight Operations and Training, with responsibility for all flight training and university air transportation. He holds two degrees from the Ohio State University: B.S. in Agriculture and M.A. in Journalism.

His first aviation book, *Instrument Flying,* was published in 1972, and continues in its third edition as one of the best-sellers in popular aviation literature. Since then, he has written five more books for pilots, and hundreds of articles and columns for aviation magazines.

Taylor began his aviation career in 1955 when he entered U.S. Air Force pilot training, and after four years on active duty continued his military activity as a reservist until retirement as a Major and Command Pilot in 1979.

Still active as a pilot and accident investigator in addition to his writing, Taylor flies frequently for business and pleasure. He and his wife live in Dublin, a suburb of Columbus, Ohio.